Gallery Books
Editor: Peter Fallon

THE HISTORY OF RAIN

Conor O'Callaghan

THE HISTORY
OF RAIN

Gallery Books

The History of Rain
is first published
simultaneously in paperback
and in a clothbound edition
on 24 September 1993.

The Gallery Press
Loughcrew
Oldcastle
County Meath
Ireland

ISBN 1 85235 116 0 (*paperback*)
     1 85235 117 9 (*clothbound*)

The Gallery Press receives financial assistance from An Chomhairle
Ealaíon / The Arts Council, Ireland.

Contents

September

It must be a cliché to think, however brief,
that light on a wall and our voices
out in the open are the pieces
we shall look upon in retrospect as a life.

There is a danger of circumstance smothering
even the smallest talk. If a breeze
shakes another colour from the trees
we say a word like *withering*

without the slightest hint of irony.
After a season of fruitful conversation
and reflective pauses in the garden
we say we know what it means to be lonely.

Today the first moment of autumn tolls
like a refrain from the nineteen thirties.
The voices of friends and courtesies
are interrupted by thunder and the radio crackles.

We shall remember it as the impending doom
and use this afternoon as an example of decay
when there is nothing left for us to say
and September has outstayed its welcome.

Today our clothes will be spoiled by rain.
We shall drag from the lawn the chairs and table
that all summer made us comfortable.
Though all of that remains to be seen.

The Last Cage House in Drogheda

Made bi Nicholas Bathe in the ieare
of ovr lord 1570 bi hiv Mor carpenter

Maybe a final order from the sheriff was sent
after the neighbours complained it was an eyesore
and, because the oak had been stolen from Mellifont,
claimed that some god had settled an old score
when the floorboards smelt and the beams were rotten.
But who lived there, and where they went, is forgotten.

All that survives is an unpeopled picture
with the first owner's inscription. It traps
in pencil on a page of mist the architecture
of a crumbling age and someone's understandable hopes
that the place where so many people once lived
would, despite the weather, be somehow saved.

Maybe the heir in a family of settlers
left instructions for the lot to be pulled down
after he returned to a different cold in Chester.
Or a pail that caught two centuries of rain
was thrown away, and with it a clatter
of tenants stepped out to freedom and squalor.

The only certainty is that one morning in Drogheda
in 1825 an amateur draughtsman turned up early,
and for half a day passers-by stopped and saw
the corner of Shop St. and Laurence St. differently.
Then tea-chests filled with earthenware and spoons
were stacked onto the cobbles in the late afternoon.

And someone alone upstairs probably recognised
history being listened to from a particular angle
for the last time, while boys whistling outside
could see no meaning in the single
martin rising from the thatch, or yellow bars
on the floor and worktop that were just wiped bare.

Say someone who had shared one room with her husband
and with her husband's friend and his nephew;
who wondered if anything that had been left behind
could be used again, and thought how the years flew;
who, with the final call, put a spray of harebells
in a jam jar on the ledge, to be gathered in the rubble.

A Bird in the House

The draught that grew softly against glass
persisted as a chaffinch
trapped in one of the back bedrooms.

We listened to it flap away a whole afternoon
after whistling and waving arms
and biscuits on the window-sill would not do.

For the umpteenth time I spoke
of the ages to come
that would care nothing for us

and would make light of our house.
I opened all the windows and doors
but still the small captivity held.

When the release descended with rain
glancing the shutters and trees
we barely noticed the wing-beats ending.

For an hour we couldn't distinguish
if what we heard was just imagined
or something remembered becoming still more distant.

Scaldie

It fell from the eaves
into the yard
in blinding rain:

the bird half-formed
in the dog's mouth
in the kitchen,

a word that just comes
out in February
and never gets very far.

The Swimming Pool

The swimming pool on the headland shuts in October,
when the gate dwindles and the lifeguard believes
it's pointless to carry on netting the water
littered with the autumnal débris of Coke cans and leaves.

I break in through the back out of season
and watch it rustle on the surface more than usual,
as if it's about to return to the surf and rain
on the far side of the turquoise wall.

Sometimes a gale or an occasional storm
shatters across the rocks, only to find
the end is never clear and the wall holds firm
despite the predictions of graffiti and the wind.

Which now and then is what makes me wander
out on a limb before another year is closed,
to reflect on the edges of a shape and to ponder
scraps of waves like phrases that are left unused.

Everything is as it was when the railed doors
were locked. Now the stile only gives
to south-westerlies that freckle the diving board
and the concrete seats. Everything and nothing moves.

The edges of the swimming pool are the last
lines visible when shapelessness comes
with evening like a fine spray and the aftertaste
of chlorine lingers from the changing rooms.

I write my name and the date with a stone,
and make it scatter gulls that disappear
into the air, and resolve once again
to learn to swim in the new year.

A tourist notice gives the distance back to town.
I say 'Will closing time continue until summer?'
to test my voice out loud across the deep end,
then leave the way I came without an answer.

Outside all of this endures a mess
of squalls and winter on the corrugated strand
where someone who couldn't care less
walks towards the torn sky and England.

In summer shapes appear more precise.
The colours of the swimming pool
are exact again, and are cemented as one place.
The sun is hardly broken, and days swell.

Mengele's House

It was considered
the finest in its street
on the outskirts of Buenos Aires.
Splashing and screams were heard
during the long July heat
in adjacent gardens.

Nobody has lived there
since the last family fled.
Now and then a researcher comes,
or a would-be buyer
armed with rosary beads
noses around the bedrooms.

Since all the glass
was kicked from a window
by legless students,
the lambency of trees
is free to come and go
in the gutted kitchen.

Out the back are piles
of twigs and compost,
a seventies lawnmower
and aquamarine tiles,
exactly as they were left
by the last owner,

who talked about himself a lot,
chatting across the fence,
but never had the neighbours
past his gate,
and never even once
darkened their doors.

In the neighbourhood
he's remembered still.
He was the old misery
who had strange kids,
a swimming pool,
and a history.

1949

Because everyone has vanished since lunch
two girls in flat summer dresses have come close by.
Though it is quite late in the year
their arms are bare in an awkward heat,
feathers are clustered on the grass.

The figures walking in the field behind
are the months that will return after September.
When the simple watercolours lined in the nursery
begin to run, and the town, visible against evening,
warps back towards the cold.

There is one particular photograph of my aunt
standing by the greenhouse in the snow.
In this a year of pain is discoloured
by her university scarf,
a flower bed wizened by the new sun.
In this again are the weekends at home:
the serious walks on the beach,
my grandfather in plus-fours, perished and hurt,
evergreens and rain clouds beneath him,
the remaining hydrangea blossoms
left to stiffen in the front room
that is only unlocked for visitors and on Saturdays.

Watching Clouds

Each time the force of cloud weathers the sky
we attempt to emulate their purpose in fire.

> Or in pulling back the window to mute the wind
> notice earlier moons brightened by a shoal of coral.

Once we left the house for the longest space
that we could find between fast clouds and midday.

> For several hours we were divided by an emerald storm
> that followed and caught us from the nearest horizon.

It separated against our arms and against our clothes.
In the end we were welcomed up to the outskirts of town.

> Now, in December, dawns stand behind pylons
> and enamel clouds. Afternoons clear to the headland

littered with fallen shells to watch a blue fleet
blown across the edges of the hemisphere.

> Two miles away we notice the doors swell and jar,
> or work on in the yard speckled by fine rain.

On Re-entering the Lavender City

On re-entering the lavender city
on a warm Christmas, I am struck
by the absence of noise. Today only
the turrets and flags remain; they break
into inaudible colour and the sky
broods on the streets where I walk.

In your house we talk again
of the Wedgwood pieces,
matching them to the afternoon.
We talk of how each design successfully
depicts a Victorian
world that would preserve every movement

as the eternal flurry into stillness;
of delft traders, disused ox-carts,
merchant ships, tea clippers.
On a day of heavy pigments,
almost completely without people,
except for two who turn from the port

and begin up even steps
to where a pattern of deserted streets
is the aftermath of some great event.
We talk of how something is lost
when we realise what we protect;
how the mountains of the world are vast

and how the city wall
is just a lilac flame,
a garland of forget-me-nots and blue roses.
We agree a storm
is necessary within that stillness
for the flags and the wind to be the same.

Although we like the way everything
of then and now is constant
in a one-hundred-year old jug:
the blown horizon, the water's end;
the way the place of blue and white things
and its finished sounds,

and their absence, all stay intact;
or returning to your house, how I find
the same instants of rest
still unbroken, while outside
a lavender sky has cracked
the evening with thin fire.

A Flight of Cranes

1

When I wrote a passage beginning
The way to the world is through trees

I wanted to find a romantic limit
where trees are bare in one perpetual season.

Something like
the flight of golden cranes
I saw by chance today

on nineteenth century silk.

Something blown from completion into wings
and air, or a hundred years
of hesitancy lifting outwards
from a square of ocean

without a sound.

2

The way to the world is through trees.
They open to a barren country
where the coastline folds as long as you wish

and it is always evening.

You walk that far to speak words
in a place where there are really none,
only the stir flight makes while it lasts.

You retrace your steps into the future
and feel the gust of cranes against your face.
You finish with the waves and the distance. That's all.

This is the new reworking of an old song.

Briefly, the spray of birds behind you
scatters outwards against silence
and the world that is inaudible.

Then you move on unchanged,
the day is almost lost.

Soon you will turn in, to warmth and rest,
having said little of what you really meant to say.

The symbols that surround you
are reliable and the same.
A road, a gate, a fire, a dream nearer than you think.

Each way of listening,

each way of hearing and not hearing,
is represented against the rush-light
of a beautiful strong sun.

The metaphors for decline
are a solitary language
and a winter tide
dissolving on a shore.

The Dream of Edward Elgar

There's a story the composer
used to tell. About weeks
in the middle of a hard winter
when insomnia, silence, and sickness
were the only prayers he could hear.
And about the evening he returned to work

until *The Dream of Gerontius* was complete,
after hearing voices outside,
and, in a downpour of sleet,
helping a neighbour bind
a blizzard of sheep
away from darkness and the road.

In a letter to a friend
some years later, he seemed
moved by the ease of it all,
by the passing sounds and the ease
with which each note fell,
almost taken to be real.

He said he thought the simple
movement was the same
as that from night-blindness to understanding shapes.
As each time, finished in the drawing-room,
he would blow against a lamp
and find himself blindfolded in a pallid gloom.

Until the last shapes of his age
separated, and night snowed
against the mirror, the cream drapes,
the notepaper, the piano,
the lampshade,
the mantelpiece, the bay window.

Landscape

It's a view that seems too familiar.
From where a gate fades into the foreground
a whole landscape stretches away between
what is already known and what is seen,
to where the earth rinses into the sky
and a town glimmers in another age.
This morning it will end a barren spell
in which drizzle and early darknesses
have obscured interiors out of reach.
At noon the kitchen table has been cleared,
windows rattle in intermittent sun,
a church bell is muffled by the distance.
Setting a fire for later in the day
and making out from the back of the house,
there is no time to pause along the way
and doubt the significance of something
known so well. The values of clarity
and perspective will only be troubled
by the afterthought of a lost ploughboy
wandering across the field of vision.
By then, weeks of sketching for one fine day
will be looked upon as a single moment.
One glance up from this point takes in a line
of chimneys and spires under wisps of smoke,
a stream of pale nineteenth century clouds,
and hedgerows extending back from the town
past a graveyard sheltered by rookeries,

to the open acres closer at hand
where the grass has been flattened by March
and where the brightness for a second
has been blustered onto another plain.

From the Opening Entries
of a Diary, March 1975

1

With the unpredicted mild weather and greater amounts of
people in town, there's been talk of a small group of us making
a nostalgic day trip to a local summer resort, and avoiding the
chaos surrounding the parade.

Recently I've come to wondering whether or not I've ended
up like him. Sometimes I think how often we saw him walk away.

2

The house belongs to people my father knew.
It looks as though it was closed two years ago
after a death everyone expected.
The curtains on the ground floor have all been drawn,
and both garages have been firmly padlocked.

In an effort to tempt prospective buyers,
the estate agents had planted several
young sycamores opposite the main entrance.
The patio is covered with newspaper
upon which there is a row of flower pots

and a curious fish-shaped vase that had been
brought from the sitting-room without permission.
The rose bed at the bottom of the garden
has developed a film of thin sand. The fire,
normally kept alive through spring, is raked clean.

Our voices seem to enter the tennis court
with a flat, anticipated suddenness.
In places the grass has grown almost a foot.
The remains of a torn net is strewn across
the top of the hedge, and the roller has been

dragged onto a more exposed stretch of the lawn.
Cast Irons, Pierce Co., Wexford, Ireland.
1947. At times it seemed wrong
to look past the niceness of someone cycling
out before tea, a drive overlooking trees.

Then yesterday evening he half-explained
what his plans would be for the bank holiday.
When we came down we were told by the barman
that he was gone since early in the morning.
After lunch we drove here along the coast. Time.

The Quay Inn is closed. The back-shore caravans
have cracked perspex and IRA scrawled in shit
to remind you not everyone forgets.
The sheds kept by the windsurfing club are closed.
The private residences are boarded up.

The souvenir shop is closed. It's quite common
to imagine that nothing ever happens.
Perhaps it's just a simple question of luck
choosing the moment to make your appearance.
You might notice that the railings at the prom

are being painted the same shade of turquoise,
that someone had dragged one of the garden seats
from the collapsed summerhouse and piled the rest
of the odds-and-ends into the potting shed
with something like the same inconspicuous,

end-of-season feeling of finality
so as not to alarm any of the others.
Ten minutes ago you saw a jet passing.
Perhaps it's obvious that an imprint left
on a part of the court under the large beech

has dried and its cracks have begun to open.
Legend has it that when the youngest daughter
finally stopped arriving home at weekends,
travellers and their children slept on the lawn.
Most nights a fire was spotted in the orchard.

At a quarter past five the wind, audible
behind an abandoned foodstore on the road,
is like music from an overhead window.
Rooms and landscapes stand between nearness and dark,
and dusk approaches from a greater distance.

The lights on the terraces farther inland
suggest there is a more blatant loneliness
in not having made the same careless mistakes.
Cheering from an early season race meeting
drifts up the estuary. You might notice

a brittle bar of *Sunlight* in the kitchen,
or the migration of dust from an open
leaflet explaining radiation treatment
on a coffee table beneath the front blinds.
Every once in a while the sea visits.

Home

Your family home is gone. On open ground I stand and say:
I am standing in the front room, in the hallway,
in the kitchen. I am standing at the foot of the stairs . . .
to continue the pretence of knowing where everything once was.

Everything now is exaggerated by an evening late in June,
the last minutes of childhood. You close the curtains
of your bedroom. For a short while you listen to the ancient
sound of your father's car running at the gate.

The History of Rain

for Johnny McCabe 1903-1993

These are the fields where rain has marched
from time to time. This is the year that
is measured in consistent downpours, until it spills
on the foreground of a basin covered, the tone of dull enamel.

In the half rush to shelter, these unripe blackberries
and woodbine drifts at the level crossing distract a generation
that knows the probability of sitting through August, the blight

of reticence raising a month past an average fall.
Or that later sees the lost patch momentarily bleached
as if by an hour of recorded sun and the history of light.

In the photograph of 1940, my granduncle and his mother.
Late that tall summer they fold their sleeves and step
into the front yard to watch a swarm of veined clouds pass.

As if the full world might still end here,
away from the horizon of more populated storms.

Forgetting that soon they will run back to the house
and the wireless babbling, and listen to the gentle clapping
on slate and galvanised roofs where the sky begins,
suddenly uncertain at the border of an even longer decade.

A Pear Tree at Knowth, Planted 1880

When he came back from the world with shells
and coloured cloth, Mr Thompson planted a pear tree
for the birth of his only daughter.
Now she is eighteen, his stories remain
in a world of Saturdays alone, her uncle
returning with news of trouble farther down the country,
the same bleak polonaise crackling at tea.
On the hill at Knowth she shows her brother
the horizons of the earth. Before spots of thunder
arrive from the midlands, and they run
for the house, their baskets forgotten,
to shelter from the falling of the imminent century.

Airstrip

A shed on the flat side of the island,
a windsock that doubles as the moon,
and thin grass rippling above where sand
and limestone fold against the ocean.
After a week of solitude, herring gulls
flock behind the house, and an engine falls
nearer through the eye of daylight.
A door bangs again, eight miles on,
and voices emerge into a grey night
from the last ten minutes of perfect vision.

Song

I built my house the wrong way round
with the outside in and the inside out.
I have been under the weather ever since,
hoping the world will make inverted sense.

The home of my dreams no longer seems likely
now the process of decay has started so quickly.
The carpet and curtains, though still quite new,
are perpetually soggy with berries and dew.

The bath and toilet can be seen from the gate,
in the upstairs bedrooms sparrows mate,
a chair from the lounge lies toppled on the lawn,
the floral wallpaper peels in the sun.

The formica is warped on the kitchen press
where a family of swallows has made its nest.
The windows are moulding, their frames are rotten,
the calendar is torn, the radio broken.

I built my house the wrong way round
and now the world seems inside out.
I convince myself that everything's clearer
when the heat goes in and the days cloud over.

Then I shelter from sudden squalls
in the room at the centre with pebble-dashed walls
and a ceiling of slates turned in from the sky
to a darkened space where no birds fly.

Poachers

The whole island
agrees they should be
ashamed of themselves,
whoever they are.

On the late walk
home, I pause
at the top of the road
and make out

between waves
the whispers
of poachers
in a boat

in the stars,
their unwise
laughter that
can't be helped.

The Ocean

We wanted to go to the ocean,
to undress and make love,
so drove across the hottest afternoon
on record, with the sun roof

wide open, to where you were sure
would be a deserted cove.
But found, miles from anywhere,
that it wasn't entirely unheard of.

We agreed to take the plunge
as far from the crowd as possible.
We dared each other to change
without once using a towel.

At one point we just lay
at the edge of the surf in togs
and tried to get carried away.
It was useless. Too many dogs,

and fathers in snorkel and flippers,
and kids playing football,
and scorched day-trippers
watching from *The Blue Yonder Hotel.*

In the end we drove home
the same evening, and arrived late
to find the kitchen and living-room
had absorbed the city's heat.

I'd say we both remember this
when something in the small hours gives,
or when a train behind the house
passes like a handful of waves.

The Swimming Pool

This is the inland silence that allows
no sounds to enter. It is also dawn.

The rockery is black with the sun behind.
Outside, the world has yet to start.

The step I take from the edge into the shallows
makes no ripples on the white day that follows.

A Large Diver

— David Hockney, 1978

The twenty-seventh and last essay
on water and light

on the human figure.
Gregory has just dived

from a July day in upstate
New York and splashed

the perception of heat as tiles
and corners and transparent shadows.

The grass will only be still,
the gravel unblemished,

for as long as he can hold his breath.
When work re-starts in another garden

and cars on the new freeway
are heard a mile from here

this second will be scattered
by ripples like gulls

and by a restlessness to break out
from paper pools, and move on.

Three Villanelles in California

1

I remember the mornings clouds came
in slabs or, like hand prints,
the marks of falling rain

hitting the coffee ads on the highway
with the same bland accent.
I remember the mornings clouds came.

I saw you once in Monterey,
your face splashed or burnt,
the marks of falling rain

that made your dress seem grey,
watching a dumb street pageant.
I remember the mornings clouds came,

our palms still marked by red clay,
the skylight in the apartment,
the marks of falling rain,

the warm bank of lies we'd say
was the edge of another continent.
I remember the mornings clouds came,
the marks of falling rain.

2

The city in which we have heard
the sales-pitch for everlasting pleasure,
the noise of advertising hoardings,

countless days of sun that covered
the pavements white, only obscures
the city in which we have heard

single afternoons touting credit cards,
almonds, the sky, flat mineral water,
the noise of advertising hoardings.

Often (the golden afterwards),
sick of cocktails and Mahler,
the city in which we have heard

pools of traffic drone, we drift towards
the outskirts and harbour,
the noise of advertising hoardings,

and sit and watch the bewildered
descent of white freighters,
the city in which we have heard
the noise of advertising hoardings.

3

At night your dreams bled,
walked out to sleep, your hair in
your mouth, your yellowing dress

matting the chair, bleached
by the fall of coastbound cars.
At night your dreams bled.

I remember how the lemon trees
in the suburbs would smear
your mouth, your yellowing dress

with shadows, warm smog beached
on to evening, the fragrant rush hour.
At night your dreams bled

in the Pacific house you guessed
would be empty. At dawn your easy sister,
your mouth, your yellowing dress

drying in gardens I thought to shed,
finally, in early summer.
At night your dreams bled,
your mouth, your yellowing dress.

Pigeons

Busty never asked me why I came around.
Twice a week we cycled to the farthest hill
to shake his pigeons from a *Marietta* box, knowing
they'd be back before us in half-light on the wall.

He was with my father, on short-term hire.
I invented messages to go and watch sheet metal
being splintered to gold. The others laughed
behind his back because he hardly spoke at all.

Then the welders were let go, and he was gone.
On the first evening of the holidays
I found his yard in tatters, the loft on its side,
the wire spattered with feathers, white and grey.

I kept trying the bell, and listened to it ring
in the hall until night built behind the town.
There was no answer. My mother told me
to sit in the front room and calm down.

He spoke its name each time he threw a pigeon
in the air and saw it broke from the initial stutter.
I felt a small heart in my palm for days after,
and my father's taunt: 'I told you he wasn't all there.'

The story goes . . . he packed his bags
and sat out all night; he was heard at dawn,
shouting and shouting; the whole of Dundalk
woke to clouds flyblown with homing pigeons.

River at Night

for Vona

We do this at least once a year.
The midges, the cow parsley, the stagnant air

are signposts to the only deep enough pool
after weeks have dried the current to a trickle.

After too much heat, and too much cider,
the night seems forever and the water inviting.

We have walked for miles into unfenced land
where the hum of the distant town is drowned,

and find again that the core of summer
is cold against our sun-burned shoulders.

There's no special way of deciding who goes first.
It just happens that my jeans and tee-shirt

have been left on parched, hoof-marked earth
where a cigarette ripens closer to your mouth.

On the other bank, an orchard and the sky's
expanse spread out like a field of fireflies.

No birdsong, nothing swaying in the high grass,
and little that ties us to what we recognise.

The silence is only disturbed by your voice
saying it can't possibly be so easy,

the planets blossoming. Only the remote throng
of cars at closing time asks if this is wrong.

To forget ourselves and a world more sober.
To forget that the slow persistence of the river

among black horses, black ragwort, black crab-apple trees
is just the brief eternity between two boundaries.

That when we walk this way in a different year
the same sense of longing will still be here.

On the surface of the universe my splashing
and your laughter scarcely make an impression.

After the silence has resumed you say that at some
point we should think of turning back. Come.

For now the night is shining on your arms.
Imagine that we've shaken off the sun and its harness.

Take off your bracelet and your black dress,
and stretch out across the confluence of two days

to where I am floating in darkness.

The Mild Night

I have taken an armchair into the garden
to enjoy the quietness at the end of May.
This is the way the mild night begins.

I have turned off the only lamp in the kitchen,
blown out the candles and put them away.
I have taken an armchair into the garden.

The lights in the trees can barely be seen
as evening comes and the land falls away.
This is the way the mild night begins.

The road past the house is lit with whitethorn
and grey poplars shine just long enough to say
I have taken an armchair into the garden.

The light on the grass, the blackening sun,
the sunflowers, the sky, the open wind all say
This is the way the mild night begins.

I have forgotten all I have said of pain
to enjoy the quietness at the end of May.
I have taken an armchair into the garden.
This is the way the mild night begins.

Different Sunflowers

Versions of a poem by Montale

1

I have been given a sunflower
that I have placed in singed ground
in a garden in the south, where the colours
of the bay and the air are shadowed by its moods.

Now what I say is only difficult
if it becomes easily said.
When I walk to the end of a room
my face and arms move into light and sound.

I have been given a shoot
that I am told will open to the noon vapours.
I have been given a sunflower
and its illusions of light.

2

I wanted to give you a sunflower
to plant in the white earth of your garden
near the coast, to turn its frown
to the reflected blues of sea and air.

I wanted you to know the complexity
of everything that seems straightforward,
that to disappear is to be lucky
like figures streaming into shade and sound.

I wanted you to have the seed of light
where living is ignored as air.
I wanted to give you a sunflower
distracted by that light.

3

Bring to my home a sunflower
so that I can plant it in soil
bittered by the sea wind, and show its yellow
face to the opposing blues of sky and water.

Eventually the obscure thing
faces back towards clarity,
and the warm limbs of shade and song
are merged into accidents of movement.

Bring me the plant of life
dispersing the mists of summer.
Bring to my home a sunflower
deranged by the sunlight.

Postcard

I've spent that last week inside,
lounging around, making a list
of all that's mine and all that's lost.
Now there's little else for me to add.

In three days I leave for good.
Everyone else keeps saying
how great it would be if I could
choose words for leaving and staying,

and manage to capture my feelings
with something not too vague or unkind.
So I've written some rhetorical questions,
said the weather's bad and nothing's changed.

I'm tired of that. Today's warm and bright.
I'm writing this lying on my parents' bed,
the blinds drawn, with daylight
between myself and the rest of the world.

Silver Birch

Here, in time, the words for trees will
be darkness's other names (lime, ash, evergreen)
and will alter what happens. Today I read
the pages where a generation falls still.

In my book the plain of Birkenau
opens into the surrounding fields
of silver birch that once sealed
it within its name . . . *from the German* . . .

The branches of the past rumble in the wind.
Some parents tell their children to go on
listening to the trees before they are gone,
that each leaf is a minute turning to the ground.

I read of the gypsy encampment near their home
and the day in October when it is lit with war.
I read of those who pass through there
for years to come, remembering their freedom.

The day is gone. My longest memory of trees
is the one in which I walk across a road
to where silver birch leaves are darkened on one side.
The shadows from a story will survive like this.

Note

page 10 *Cage house*: Tudor style timber framed house.

" . . . such cage houses (were) composed of a strong framework of oak . . . They were introduced here in several of our towns during the reigns of Henry VIII and Elizabeth . . . " 'On Irish Half-Timbered Houses', by W. Frazer, *The Journal of the Royal Society of Antiquaries in Ireland*, vol. 21, page 367, 1891.

" . . . at Drogheda, Co. Louth, there were many picturesque timber cage-work houses . . . a drawing of the last wooden house of note (was) made shortly before its demolition in 1825 . . . Throughout Ireland wooden houses have now totally vanished though they were once numerous; indeed 16th century Dublin consisted mainly of cage-work houses. They suffered severely from the weather (Ireland being damper than England) and as they were seldom owner-occupied did not receive the regular maintenance they needed." *The Houses of Ireland*, by Brian de Breffny and Rosemary ffolliott, page 26. Thames and Hudson, 1975.

Acknowledgements

Acknowledgements are due to the editors of the following publications where many of these poems first appeared: *Ambit*, *The Honest Ulsterman*, *The Irish Times*, *Krino*, *Lines Review*, *The North*, *Orbis*, *Oxford Poetry*, *Poetry Ireland Review*, *The Rialto*, *The Steeple*, and *Verse*.

Selections appeared in *12 Bar Blues* (Raven Introductions) and *The Cloverdale Anthology*.

Thanks are also due to An Chomhairle Ealaíon / The Arts Council, Ireland, for a bursary received in 1990.